MICHIGAN

A PHOTOGRAPHIC PORTFOLIO

MICHIGAN
A PHOTOGRAPHIC PORTFOLIO

FEATURING THE PHOTOGRAPHY OF

DAVID MUENCH
CARR CLIFTON
TERRY DONNELLY
FRED HIRSCHMANN
WILLARD CLAY
TOM TILL
JEFF GNASS
STEVE MULLIGAN
IAN ADAMS

BROWNTROUT PUBLISHERS, INC.
SAN FRANCISCO

Lake Superior edge, Pictured Rocks National Lakeshore
DAVID MUENCH

MICHIGAN: A PHOTOGRAPHIC PORTFOLIO features the
finest photographs of Michigan by a distinguished group
of landscape photographers. Captions for the
photographs were provided by the photographers.

Photographs, Captions © 1995
David Muench, Carr Clifton, Terry Donnelly,
Fred Hirschmann, Willard Clay, Tom Till, Jeff Gnass,
Steve Mulligan, Ian Adams

LIBRARY OF CONGRESS
CATALOGING-IN-PUBLICATION DATA

Michigan, a photographic portfolio.
        p.   cm.
    ISBN 1-56313-760-7 (hardcover : alk. paper)
    ISBN 1-56313-761-5 (softcover : alk. paper)
    1. Michigan—Pictorial works. 2. Wilderness areas—
Michigan—Pictorial works.
F567.M533   1995   95-22535
977.4—dc20   CIP

Printed and bound by
Dai Nippon Printing Company, Ltd., Hong Kong

10 9 8 7 6 5 4 3 2 1

Arc of Northern Lights over Union Bay of Lake Superior,
Porcupine Mountains Wilderness State Park, Upper Peninsula
FRED HIRSCHMANN

INTRODUCTION

THE TWO PENINSULAS that make up the state of Michigan perfectly represent the opposing aspects of the state. The Upper Peninsula is a heavily forested wilderness of lake and mountain while the Lower has largely been converted by the hand of man into one of the most productive agricultural and industrial areas in the world. Within both generalizations there are startling exceptions, of course. Sleeping Bear Dunes on Lake Michigan in the Lower is a well-preserved example of the ancient shorelines of that great Ice Age lake while the city of Sault St. Marie and the Soo Canal constitute an essential commercial corridor in the Upper. Nevertheless, Michiganders seem very pleased to have two Michigans, one rooted in everyday reality, the other a place to escape to if only in daydreams.

Nature photography in Michigan begins with the Great Lakes of Superior, Michigan, and Huron which surround and divide the state. The state's purest wilderness is actually found within the lakes, on Isle Royale and the Manitou Islands. The north shore of the Upper Peninsula is the most photogenic area of all, where the Porcupine Mountains, the Keweenaw Peninsula, and Pictured Rocks National Lakeshore define the primeval coastline of the largest freshwater lake in North America. In addition, Michigan has over 11,000 other lakes that are dotted with 500 islands, big and small. The interior of the state early surrendered vast expanses of forest to the plow but even in the south conservation efforts and wise land use have resulted in the preservation of almost 4,000,000 acres of woodland.

This book looks only at the naturally beautiful in this variegated landscape. Our view is not only myopic, it is also selective. Photography is a medium of communication where the story told need not be the whole truth, but where everything shown must be wholly truthful. Uniquely centered in the heart of North America, Michigan presents to photographers a unique challenge: to portray the singular beauty of the North Woods and the Great Lakes still extant in the late twentieth century. Our collection of images is intended to reflect that endeavor.

Lake Michigan shore, Straits of Mackinac
DAVID MUENCH

Lake of the Clouds, sunrise, Porcupine Mountains Wilderness State Park
DAVID MUENCH

Tahquamenon Falls State Park
DAVID MUENCH

Fireweed *(Epilobium angustifolium)*, Ottawa National Forest
WILLARD CLAY

Late sun on the dunes, grasses and frozen shoreline of Lake Michigan, Muskegon State Park
TERRY DONNELLY

Bond Falls, Ottawa National Forest
WILLARD CLAY

Wave polished beach cobbles on the shore of Lake Superior between Maple Creek and Black River
FRED HIRSCHMANN

Autumn colors of sugar maples and red sumac along the Presque Isle River, Porcupine Wilderness State Park
FRED HIRSCHMANN

Beach rocks, Rock Harbor, Isle Royale National Park
STEVE MULLIGAN

Hemlock trunks, Black River Gorge
DAVID MUENCH

Iron ore bearing Jasper rock, Lake Superior
TOM TILL

Icy winter stream, Ottawa National Forest
TOM TILL

Details of red maple leaves and moss above the Black River
between Potawatomi and Gorge Falls, Ottawa National Forest
FRED HIRSCHMANN

Dusk over Lake Michigan, Miners Castle, Pictured Rocks National Lakeshore
FRED HIRSCHMANN

Sugar maple bough and tilted trunks, Hiawatha National Forest
JEFF GNASS

Lake of the Clouds, Porcupine Mountains Wilderness State Park
WILLARD CLAY

Beach grass and sand
patterns at Aral Dunes
on Lake Michigan,
Empire Bluffs in distance,
Sleeping Bear Dunes
National Lakeshore
JEFF GNASS

Large basalt block below Sturgeon Falls in Sturgeon River Gorge
JEFF GNASS

Autumn colors along the Carp River, Porcupine Mountains Wilderness State Park
FRED HIRSCHMANN

Winter trees silhouetted on a stony ridge, Leelanau County
TERRY DONNELLY

Hoary Puccoon (*Lithospermum canescens*) and driftwood on dune, P.J. Hoffmaster State Park
TERRY DONNELLY

Sunset clouds over Lake Michigan from North Bar Lake,
Sleeping Bear Dunes National Lakeshore
TERRY DONNELLY

Brilliant red sugar maple leaves in autumn, beach cobbles on
the shore of Lake Superior, Ottawa National Forest
FRED HIRSCHMANN

Yellow Lady's Slippers *(Cypripedium calceolus)*, Upper Peninsula
WILLARD CLAY

Sunrise over Lake of the Clouds, glacier-carved landscape, Porcupine Mountains Wilderness State Park
FRED HIRSCHMANN

Lake Huron, Presque Isle County
IAN ADAMS

Lake Huron, Presque Isle County
IAN ADAMS

Along the Jordan River in the Jordan River Wilderness, Antrim County
IAN ADAMS

Shore grasses, Lake Michigan, Wilderness State Park
TOM TILL

Evening light at Sturgeon Bay, Wilderness State Park, Emmet County
IAN ADAMS

Cascade, Presque Isle River, Porcupine Mountains Wilderness State Park
DAVID MUENCH

Dune grass, Grand Sable Dunes, Pictured Rocks National lakeshore
DAVID MUENCH

Mixed hardwoods, Porcupine
Mountains Wilderness State Park
CARR CLIFTON

41

Wagner Falls flowing in forest, Wagner Falls State Park
TERRY DONNELLY

Brook cascading into Lake Superior,
Pictured Rocks National Lakeshore
CARR CLIFTON

43

Winter tree patterns on sky and snow-covered hillside, Leelanau County
TERRY DONNELLY

Dwarf dogwood, Pictured Rocks National Lakeshore
CARR CLIFTON

Sleeping Bear Dunes from the beach at North Bar Lake,
Sleeping Bear Dunes National Lakeshore
TERRY DONNELLY

Sunset afterglow on weathered ice floes and chunks on the Lake Michigan shoreline, Muskegon State Park
TERRY DONNELLY

Large white pine frames Pere Marquette River, Manistee National Forest
JEFF GNASS

Lakeport State Park, Lake Huron
STEVE MULLIGAN

Afternoon light on Miners Castle, Pictured Rocks National Lakeshore
WILLARD CLAY

Wave washed beach pebbles, Whitefish Point, Lake Superior shore
FRED HIRSCHMANN

Birch tree along Lake Superior, Pictured Rocks National Lakeshore
CARR CLIFTON

Manabezho Falls, Presque Isle River Scenic Area, Porcupine Mountains Wilderness State Park
JEFF GNASS

Maple leaves in potholes, Manido Falls on the Presque Isle River, Porcupine Mountains Wilderness State Park
FRED HIRSCHMANN

Pool with rocks on shore of Lake Michigan, Nordhouse Dunes
Wilderness, Manistee National Forest
WILLARD CLAY

Rapids, Presque Isle River, Porcupine Mountains Wilderness State Park
DAVID MUENCH

Venus and crescent moon at dusk above forest near Hurricane River, Pictured Rocks National Lakeshore
FRED HIRSCHMANN

Munising Falls along
North Country National Scenic Trail,
Pictured Rocks National Lakeshore
JEFF GNASS

Dunes and reeds reflected on the calm surface of North Bar Lake at sunset,
Sleeping Bear Dunes National Lakeshore
TERRY DONNELLY

Beach rocks, Whitefish Point, Lake Superior shore
FRED HIRSCHMANN

Mount Fuller, Warren Dunes State Park, Berrien County
STEVE MULLIGAN

Birch tree in pine forest with summer ferns, Sleeping Bear Dunes National lakeshore
TERRY DONNELLY

Storm reflection, Tahquamenon River
DAVID MUENCH

A winter storm prepares to blot out the sun at Tawas Point State Park along Lake Huron, Iosco County
IAN ADAMS

Fierce winds on Lake Superior, Pictured Rocks National lakeshore
CARR CLIFTON

New snow accents young American beech and red pine trees, North Country National Scenic Trail, Tahquamenon Falls State Park

JEFF GNASS

Stream, Lake Superior State Forest, Schoolcraft County
IAN ADAMS

Winter moonrise, Lake Gogebic State Park
TOM TILL

Hardwoods and the Carp River,
Porcupine Mountains Wilderness
State Park
CARR CLIFTON

White birch *(Betula paprifera)* on a wooded, snow-covered dune, Nordhouse Dunes Wilderness Area, Manistee National Forest

TERRY DONNELLY

Foggy dunes, Warren Dunes State Park
TERRY DONNELLY

Beach grasses and snow dusted dunes at mouth of Miner's River, Pictured Rocks National Lakeshore
TERRY DONNELLY

Lakeside marsh, Sturgeon Bay, Lake Michigan Wilderness State Park
DAVID MUENCH

Shoreline driftwood, Crisp Point, Lake Superior
FRED HIRSCHMANN

Maple leaves, Porcupine Mountains Wilderness State Park
TOM TILL

Mosaic of maple branches and pine trunks,
Nordhouse Dunes Wilderness, Manistee National Forest
JEFF GNASS

Cloud reflection,
Tahquamenon Falls State Park
DAVID MUENCH

Fresh snow on an open pine, beech, and birch forest, Leelanau County
TERRY DONNELLY

Munising Falls, Pictured Rocks National Lakeshore
WILLARD CLAY

Pebble-covered shore at Miners Beach,
Pictured Rocks National Lakeshore
WILLARD CLAY

Silhouetted trees on dune rim, sunset over Lake Michigan, P.J. Hoffmaster State Park
TERRY DONNELLY

Detail view of multi-colored maple leaves, Hiawatha National Forest
TERRY DONNELLY

Presque Isle River Scenic
Area, Porcupine Mountains
Wilderness State Park
JEFF GNASS

Birch trunks and fall-colored forest, Pictured Rocks National Lakeshore
CARR CLIFTON

Rock Harbor, Isle Royale National Park
STEVE MULLIGAN

Blue water of Lake Superior and sand patterns of Grand Sable Dunes
TERRY DONNELLY

Detail of beach grass, driftwood, and fall-colored leaves, Pictured Rocks National Lakeshore
TERRY DONNELLY

Autumn reflections and water designs below a cascade on Black River,
Ottawa National Forest

JEFF GNASS

Moon rising over bog near Clarkston, northern Oakland County
FRED HIRSCHMANN

Blowing sand and breaking surf at
Grand Sable Dunes, Lake Superior,
Pictured Rocks National Lakeshore
JEFF GNASS

Still pool of the Presque Isle River,
Porcupine Mountains Wilderness
State Park

TERRY DONNELLY

Snow bank patterns on thawing wetlands, Blacksmith Bayou,
Manistee National Forest

TERRY DONNELLY

Grand Portal Point on Lake Superior, Pictured Rocks National lakeshore
CARR CLIFTON

Autumn-fringed leaves surround an American beech trunk, Sleeping Bear Dunes National Lakeshore
JEFF GNASS

Beach detail of stones, fall-colored leaves and pine needles,
Pictured Rocks National Lakeshore

TERRY DONNELLY

Birch trunks and maple boughs, Porcupine Mountains Wilderness State Park
JEFF GNASS

Windswept snow on dunes, Sleeping Bear Dunes National Lakeshore
TERRY DONNELLY

Sandstone cliffs of Lake Superior, Pictured Rocks National Lakeshore
CARR CLIFTON

Woods on the snow-covered bluff above Hinton Creek, Manistee National Forest
TERRY DONNELLY

Patch of Spring Beauty *(Claytonia virginica)* near the Log Slide, Pictured Rocks National Lakeshore
WILLARD CLAY

Wind-whipped waves on Lake Superior
CARR CLIFTON

Red sunset and winter sky
over Lake Michigan, Warren
Dunes State Park
TERRY DONNELLY